DEMYSTIFYING PERSONAL EVANGELISM

By Moishe Rosen

A Purple Pomegranate Pocket Book

BV
3790
.R67
1992
c.2

Copyright 1992
by Purple Pomegranate Productions,
80 Page Street, San Francisco, CA 94102.

First Edition
All rights reserved. For reprint permission, please
write to Purple Pomegranate Productions,
Permissions Department, 80 Page Street,
San Francisco, CA 94102.

Cover art by Pavel Bosak

Library of Congress Catalog
Card Number 92-32676 CIP

Rosen, Moishe, 1932-
    Demystifying Personal Evangelism / by Moishe
Rosen. — 1st ed.
        p.   cm.
    ISBN 1-881022-01-3
    1. Evangelistic work.
    2. Witness bearing (Christianity).
I. Title.
BV3790.R668   1992
248' .5—dc20   92-32676
CIP

Contents

"Not by might, nor by power, but by My Spirit says the Lord"
—*Zechariah 4:6.*

Introduction

What happens when a person accepts Christ as Savior? Is it a decision? A process? A feeling? A change of heart? How does it occur? What brings a person to commit himself or herself to God?

We do not really know the answer. We can quote Scripture. We can invite a friend to church. We can lead a person to say the right words in a prayer of repentance. Yet how conversion happens still mystifies us.

An evangelist cannot **will** a person into believing. A Christian cannot **prod** a non-believer into accepting Christ. No formula will **make** a person a Christian. How conversion transpires is a mystery. As the German theologian Dietrich Bonhoeffer put it, "The harvest is great, but **only** Jesus in His mercy can see it."

Only the Holy Spirit can woo a person to the point of making a commitment. How God uses believers in the witnessing process, even with our flaws and shortcomings, is part of the mystery. Therefore, the question is: "How do we move forward in witnessing even though there is an inherent mystique about it?"

As I prepared to write about how to demystify personal evangelism, I read several pieces of literature on witnessing. To my surprise, although the authors offer some good thoughts, none of them actually tells the reader <u>how to lead a person</u> <u>through repentance into a personal relationship</u> <u>with God</u>. Furthermore, many of the writings contain so many warnings and negative over-tones that they discourage the reader from try-ing to witness. They add to the mystery of evan-gelism rather than simplify it.

Thankfully, in my personal experience with evangelism and teaching others how to witness, I have found that we can cut through the mys-tique. **We can demystify personal evangelism.** Telling others about Christ can be easy and enjoyable.

If you have ever felt frustrated in witness-ing, then I have written this booklet for you. If you have ever had problems initiating evange-lism, then this is for you. Even if you feel com-fortable telling others about Christ, these insights may help you become more effective.

I have written this as a guide to show you how to take the first step in sharing the good news of Jesus with another person. At Jews for Jesus we primarily contact unbelieving Jews to tell them about Y'shua (the Jewish way to say Jesus). However, every person you know and meet (Jew and Gentile) needs to hear about Christ. I want to encourage you to plant many seeds. Then watch God grow those seeds and bring in the harvest.

Whom would you like to tell about Jesus Christ right now? Do you have a friend, a brother or sister, maybe a neighbor who needs to accept Christ as Savior?

What have you said to him or her about Jesus? Does he know that you believe in Christ? Have you read the Bible with him? Have you prayed with him? Have you ever asked him if he is ready to pray to commit his life to Christ?

Most important: Are these questions scaring you or convicting you?

Christians have a way of finding so many reasons not to witness. In fact, we have built up such a stockpile of excuses that they have become myths we turn to anytime we feel uneasy about speaking out—anytime we want a reason not to do it.

Before we get to the actual steps of witnessing, let's unravel some of these myths:

Myth Number One: If the person doesn't respond to my witness, it must be because I haven't properly presented the gospel.

People do not naturally give their lives to Christ. They hold on to the reins as long as possible. Therefore, we should expect resistance. We can present the gospel in exactly the right way, yet still have it rejected. Other times we can fumble through our words and forget a scripture or two, yet find that in spite of our mistakes the person wants to accept Christ as Savior.

Besides, there really is no "right way" to present the gospel. Some methods may work better than others. And, certainly, knowing doctrine helps. But God approaches each person as an individual. We must also do this when we witness. Therefore, what might have been right in witnessing to one person may not be right in witnessing to the next.

Myth Number Two: It takes time for a person to discover the truth of the gospel.

Sometimes it takes a person a long time to "come to faith," but usually it doesn't. A person often realizes his or her need for a savior after taking a personal inventory. This happens because the Holy Spirit touches that person's heart. Someone else may have planted the gospel seed long before we came along—maybe someone who thought he had failed.

Myth Number Three: If I am to be effective in evangelism, I must know the Bible very well.

Bible knowledge helps, but God doesn't require that we have a certain number of verses memorized before we can witness. He will direct what we say. In fact, often we will find that we know more than the person to whom we witness—and more than we thought we knew. Furthermore, we usually end up learning much about Christ as we tell others about Him. The section in this booklet on how to use the Gospel of John provides enough direction to get started.

Myth Number Four: I am not very good with words. It would be easier and more effective if I would just pray for the person.

We should pray. Yet if we want only to pray, how do we explain Romans 10:14? "How then shall they call on Him in whom they have not believed? And how shall they believe in Him of whom they have not heard? And how shall they hear without a preacher?"

How does the Great Commission in Mark 16:15-16 apply to us? "And He said to them [His disciples], 'Go into all the world and preach the gospel to every creature. He who believes and is baptized will be saved; but he who does not believe will be condemned.'"

It is our responsibility to tell others about Jesus whether we speak eloquently or not. Some of the most powerful witnesses make terrible spokespeople. Yet God chooses them.

Myth Number Five: Instead of witnessing, I can invite my friends to church. They will hear a sermon on sin and repentance there. After all, it is the pastor's responsibility to be an evangelist.

The pastor may be a good evangelist; however, the Great Commission doesn't call upon us "to go into all the world and invite people to church." The Great Commission calls upon us to proclaim that Jesus Christ wants to be Lord and Savior of everyone.

The Bible says, "Let the redeemed of the Lord say so." Our personal testimony adds much to our witness. It shows what God can do in a person's life.

Myth Number Six: The person will probably ask questions that I can't answer. This will prevent me from being a good witness.

No, it won't. Just tell the person that you can't answer the question right then. Make a note of it and get back to him later. Too many Christians fear not knowing all the answers. Remember, only God knows everything.

Myth Number Seven: Since God knows who will and will not accept Him—it is all predestined—I can't really make a difference.

Some people teach that God predetermines salvation, others say that He does not. Either way, we should witness. If indeed God predestines a person's eternal destination, then He not only predestines the end, but He selects the means by which that person will hear the gospel. If He has not predestined salvation, a person must still hear the gospel from someone. We have the privilege of being obedient to the Lord and perhaps being part of another person's eternal destiny whether or not

God predestines it.

Myth Number Eight: I should only witness when the Holy Spirit leads me to witness.

He already has led us to witness. Jesus said, "Go into all the world." He said, "Go to every creature." So what are we waiting for—a special revelation? Just believe and obey what Jesus said in the Bible.

Myth Number Nine: My testimony is rather dull. I know God loves me and has saved me, but nothing very dramatic has happened in my life. Will people really want to have what I have?

Does God not answer prayer? Do we not love Him? Has He not made a difference in how we live? Then should we not be willing to tell others of our love for the Lord, the prayers He has answered and how real He is? Our testimony does not have to appear in a Christian magazine or book, just in our hearts.

Myth Number Ten: I want to become friends with unbelievers. I will let them see Jesus in me. Then, when they show an interest, I will witness.

We should become friends with unbelievers. We should at least behave in a friendly, non-threatening manner toward unbelievers. However, with what is sometimes called "friendship evangelism" we end up waiting for the other person to initiate conversation about God. Too often they never ask.

Many Christians correctly note that we will find openings to evangelism when we become friends with unbelievers. We must, however, be aware of a potential pitfall. Unbelievers may or may not notice a difference in us. They will likely realize that we don't do certain things such as swearing, cheating and lying. Hopefully they will also notice a cheerfulness, a compassion and a love they don't see elsewhere. They may notice these attributes, but that doesn't necessarily mean that they want them or understand them. Even if they do desire something we have, that doesn't mean that they have the nerve to seek it, especially if it means giving up some sin they truly enjoy.

Jewish comedian Sam Levinson was right when he observed, "People don't look for God any more than a hooky-player looks for a truant officer." Most people don't seek salvation. We must go to them to tell them about it.

When I was an unbeliever, I knew many Christians. They were so afraid they would offend me that none of them ever tried to tell me about Jesus. With such friends, I could have ended up lost for all eternity!

Myth Number Eleven: I am responsible for the eternal destiny of the person to whom I am witnessing.

While we might never admit it out loud, subconsciously many of us carry blame and shame. We feel that somehow if we just say the right words, the person will believe. Worse yet, we feel that because we didn't say the right words or didn't witness soon enough or didn't pray hard enough, we failed. We accept the shame of a person's rejecting Christ and the blame of the possibility of them spending eternity in hell.

We must leave the "blame baggage" at Calvary where the crucifixion heaped all the shame of sin on Y'shua. Yes, we will make mistakes in witnessing. Therefore, even in evangelism we must learn to accept the forgiveness Y'shua provides through the resurrection where the stain of sin was removed. Only as we accept this free gift in **all** areas of our life can we become effective in showing others how they too can obtain forgiveness.

We go and tell others about salvation, but God convicts and converts the unsaved.

Chapter Two
Witnessing Principles

Do you remember when you were a teenager? Most of us suffered through growing pains. Some were physical, others emotional. We made mistakes, but hopefully we learned from them.

A child doesn't choose to mature physically. His body follows a genetic code that has set a pattern. Only disease or intentional harm can stunt natural physical development.

In adolescence, however, a child reaches a crossroads in his emotional growth. He finds that he wants to be what his friends want him to be rather than what his parents want him to be. He wants his peers to accept him even though they don't know how they should behave or how to become adults. The teenager faces a tough emotional struggle.

Just as each stage of human development has growing pains, spiritual expansion has moments of awkwardness and anxiety. **As you begin to witness, you will discover them.** Some will occur naturally, others we place upon ourselves.

Very few believers automatically want to conform to the image of Christ, whose character set the pattern for what we should be. We would rather our friends and co-workers accept us. If we succumb to this inclination, we become more like our unbelieving friends than they become like us or like God. We thereby lose the impetus to witness to them.

How do we move through the "adolescent

phase" of witnessing? How do we become what we should become rather than conform to the world? How do we witness as Christ wants us to witness rather than in a way the world accepts? Here are some basic principles we can follow:

Principle #1: **Acknowledge Christ's position as your Lord and Savior.** Christ Jesus should be the primary person to whom a believer relates. When we link up with the Almighty, His Holy Spirit flows through us, not only revealing all truth but strengthening us to act upon it. Before we can tell others about Christ, we must know Him.

Our allegiance to God must be absolute. It is experiential, not experimental. We can't "try it for a while to see if it works." When regeneration registers in our hearts and minds, a stunning reality accompanies it: God is sovereign. <u>He rules our lives.</u> The words of Jesus in Matthew 10:37 strike a solemn note: "He who loves father or mother more than Me is not worthy of Me."

This total commitment to a sovereign God provides a solid foundation for witnessing and every aspect of life.

Principle #2: **Appreciate your relationship with God.** "To appreciate" means "to add value." When a financial investment accumulates, we say it "appreciates." In the same way, when a person invests his life in the Lord, his life increases in value to the person, to God and to anyone who relates to the person.

Another way to say this would be, "Don't take God for granted." Understand that He has literally transformed us. Acknowledge that we would not be who we are without Him and His love for us. Confess that we cannot accomplish much of eternal value except that He chooses to work through us.

When someone helps us out of a jam or invites us over for dinner or helps us move from one home to another, we appreciate his or her effort. To show our thankfulness we may send a card or telephone them as a kind gesture.

We have Mother's Day to appreciate our mothers and Father's Day for our fathers. But how often do we show our heavenly Father that we appreciate all He has done? Only as we do this continually can we proceed with effective witnessing.

Principle #3: **Accept God's priorities as your priorities.** God has a divine plan that involves each of us. We can look in awe at the fact that the King of the universe, the ruler of all that ever has been or will be, has deigned to love us and use us. Once we accept and begin moving in this awesome reality, we will go, grow and glow for the Lord.

This plan involves witnessing. In Acts 1:8, Jesus did not say to His disciples, "I would **appreciate** it if you would witness." He didn't say, "Stay at Jerusalem until the coming of the Holy Spirit, then I **suggest** that you branch out from there." No, He was much firmer. He said that they should wait to receive the baptism of the Holy Spirit. Then they **would be** witnesses to Jerusalem and the entire world.

Just as a child cannot stop his legs from growing,

we cannot say that we will not witness. If a child grows naturally, his legs will be longer at age 18 than they were at age two. Likewise, If we grow according to God's spiritual pattern, we will tell others about our faith. If a child chooses not to eat the right food and not exercise, it diminishes his growth. Likewise, when we choose to disobey God's spiritual laws, it weakens our witness.

Bible reading, prayer and fellowship nourish the body and strengthen the soul. However, only evangelism is reproductive. Similar to physical exercise, witnessing may involve stretching and straining, but eventually we experience the joy of producing and reproducing.

Principle #4: **Take the gospel to the Jew first.** Paul wrote his letter to the Romans 30 years after the resurrection of Y'shua. The gospel had already gone into the world. It was well established among Jews and Gentiles. Therefore, Paul must have puzzled this non-Jewish church when he wrote:

> I am not ashamed of the gospel, because it is the power of God for the salvation of everyone who believes: first for the Jew, then for the Gentile. There will be trouble and distress for every human being who does evil: first for the Jew, then for the Gentile; but glory, honor and peace for everyone who does good: first for the Jew, then for the Gentile. (NIV)

What does it mean to go to the Jew first? When God became a man, He could have chosen any people, any place, any time. He didn't choose Oslo, Istanbul or Karachi. He chose Bethlehem, close to Jerusalem in the land of Judea. God did not have His directions or destination confused. He determined that the gospel should go to the Jews first—the people whom He had prepared as part of His plan of world redemption.

Does Paul merely give a history lesson when he says the gospel must first go to the Jews? No, he advocates a method and a model.

God appointed Paul as the "Apostle to the Gentiles." Nonetheless, whenever Paul visited a city with a Jewish population, he went straight to the synagogue. Was the Apostle confused? Was he deliberately picking quarrels? Is that the way to proclaim Christ? No, Paul taught by example and precept that the gospel should go to the Jew first as a priority.

Perhaps Paul realized that if we start with the easy part of a job, the task grows more difficult and we might be tempted to discontinue. On the other hand, if we tackle the difficult portion first, the task only becomes easier.

If we prepare to witness to Jewish people, we prepare for possible resistance. Jews often call a gentle, loving and considerate proclamation of the gospel "proselytizing—forcing your religion upon us."

Evangelization of Jewish people can lead to

confrontation. We therefore ought to develop an orientation that enables us to be champions for Jesus. This prepares us to face almost any situation.

Principle #5: **Planting and harvesting.** The basic principle is rather simple: If we plant seeds, we will have a harvest. As in agriculture, the more we sow, the more we will reap. In evangelism, we sow gospel seeds and reap souls of men and women.

To understand this principle we can look at the celebration of Pentecost. This was the festival of harvest, but it was also a time of healing.

Early Christians were celebrating Pentecost in the Upper Room when the Holy Spirit moved among them. They began to speak many different languages—and the others understood! This was a healing of what happened hundreds of years earlier in Babel.

The people at Babel sought to make a name for themselves. They were full of envy, pride and greed. God judged them by scattering them to the ends of the earth. He gave them the curse of tongues or languages so they could not understand one another.

Centuries later, people went out from the Upper Room into the streets, speaking the different languages. To some, they sounded as if they were babbling, but they were talking about God. Their words of praise were like scattered seed.

Some observers said, "They are drunk." Others said, "They are declaring the wonderful works of

God." Those who mocked had hardened hearts so they could not hear what was said. However, more than 5,000 listened and believed!

Too many Christians plant only one seed, then wait to see if it will bring a harvest before they commit to sowing. If a sprout doesn't grow from that seed, they say sowing gospel seeds is not worthwhile. If a sprout emerges from that one seed, the person may be discouraged because he has only one soul in the harvest. As important as each soul is, if we want to reach the ends of the earth, we must sow much gospel seed.

Christians attempt to witness, but become discouraged and quit when they don't see immediate results. We must sow knowing that most of the people will not immediately receive Y'shua into their hearts. Some seed will fall on hard ground, some will be snatched away by birds, but some seed will find good ground. There is a season between sowing and harvesting. This calls for patience. We sow. God gives the increase.

When Jews for Jesus began in 1973, we would hand-deliver 1,000 tracts and receive seven responses or reactions. Today that has decreased to three responses out of every 1,000 tracts distributed.

On a busy street corner it takes a missionary two hours to hand out 1,000 tracts. We can't think of anything else we could do that would be more effective in reaching Jewish people with the gospel.

Principle #6: **Declare yourself early.** Let people know you are different and why you are different.

Tell them right away so they know that you believe in Christ as the Messiah and that you intend to tell them about Him. To fly under a false flag is wrong.

I always bring up my Jewishness at the outset of a relationship. If the people don't want to be friends with me because I am Jewish, they don't have to. Likewise, if they don't want to be friends with me because I am an evangelical Christian, they don't have to.

Some believers who crave acceptance water down their message. This leaves the listener—the person to whom we witness—with a fuzzy image of who Christ is.

We must make clear our intent to evangelize the person. If we allow the person to think that we will not witness to him or her, it diminishes the perceived value of a relationship with Jesus Christ.

I would rather people think of me as a friendly fanatic who seeks every opportunity to bring Christ into a conversation than a friendly person who just happens to be a believer in Jesus. Will such an eagerness to share the gospel isolate us from others? No. I have found that it actually draws unbelievers to me.

Some people grudgingly take on certain tasks because of a sense of duty. They moan when they pay their bills, they grumble when they pay their taxes, and they sigh when an elderly person drives slowly ahead of them on the highway.

Other people do their duty, but without resentment. They joyfully write a check to VISA, happily fill out their IRS forms and gladly wait for others.

In witnessing, we must understand duty and sincerity. Sometimes we will exuberantly tell others about Christ; at other times we will not feel like telling anyone about anything!

We need to be careful. <u>Christians often feel compelled to do everything out of a pure heart.</u> We sometimes wait to witness until we feel right about it. This can be a stumbling block. Usually such people spend too much time examining their motives rather than doing their duty. We have to pay our bills and taxes whether we resent it or feel good about it! The same is true of witnessing!

Accept that you will probably feel a bit clumsy when you first want to witness. It is natural. It is as natural as nervousness before your first date with the opposite sex, apprehension about going to a new school or jitters before starting a new job. All new experiences make us feel awkward, but nobody stayed in the sixth grade simply because of the awkwardness he or she might have felt going into junior high. We just accept the "butterflies" and dive into the new experience.

It helps to begin evangelism with great expectations. Paul E. Little wrote in *How to Give Away Your Faith* (InterVarsity Press), "Every person I have known who has been used of God in personal evangelism has had an attitude of expectancy to discover interested people. In any group of people or in conversation with any particular individual he asks himself the question, 'Lord, is this one in whom you are working?' and then, as the Spirit gives opportunity, he proceeds to see what the response is."

We don't know how people will respond. So, remember that we don't preach ourselves or our worthiness, but Jesus Christ—for He is worthy. Second Corinthians 4:7 makes this clear: "But we have this treasure in earthen vessels, that the excellence of the power may be of God and not of us." Confidence in witnessing comes first in knowing that we are right in our actions, then grows as we act in a responsible and reasonable way.

After the initial apprehension, people usually feel a certain amount of satisfaction that they've done the right thing in witnessing, no matter how the person responds.

How do we start witnessing? Approach every relationship and interaction as an opportunity.

That means we have dozens of witnessing possibilities each day.

Witness With a "WOW!"

To get a conversation started, try what I call the "WOW!" approach. Y'shua used it. Consider John 4 where He was sitting by a well. Along came a woman whom He asked for a drink of water. She taunted Him about the prejudice of the Jews toward Samaritans. He responded by saying, "If you knew who it was that was asking you, you would ask of that person and He would give you rivers of living water."

The woman at the well mocked, "Well, why don't you just go ahead and give me this water so that I don't have to come here anymore?"

Jesus didn't flinch. Instead, He used the glib exchange as a catapult into a serious talk about her spiritual life. Likewise, we can throw out off-handed remarks that a person can latch onto as a conversational handle.

For example, next time you pick up your dry cleaning, try saying, "Good, but it's not as clean as Jesus can make each soul."

A person stops and asks the way to Interstate 4. Give him the directions, smile and say, "If you're looking for the way to God, Jesus said, 'I am the way, the truth and the life.'"

A non-Christian friend tells you a bit of gossip about who did what to whom. You can respond, "The Bible tells the truth when it says, 'All have sinned and come short of the glory of God.'"

A friend invites you out for dinner and asks what restaurant you prefer. You can say, "I'm going to be eating the bread of life and drinking the living waters for all eternity. You choose where we eat tonight."

To a gas station attendant you can say, "God's power is through the Holy Spirit and He can fill you in an instant."

When you use the "WOW!" approach, it will surprise the person, no doubt. This is not typical, mundane, everyday conversation. Neither is it characteristic hellfire-and-brimstone evangelism.

The person will usually respond in one of three ways: 1) Not wanting to talk to you about such things, he will smile and go on as if you didn't say it; 2) He will say he also believes in Christ; or 3) He will enter into a discussion.

Even if he or she taunts or teases you, be sure to end the exchange with a smile.

The "WOW!" approach is not persuasive. It's an invitation to talk about spiritual things.

The Bolder the Better

While the "WOW!" approach works well with casual acquaintances, we can be bolder with a friend, a neighbor or a family member. A direct challenge will get his or her attention and usually evoke a response.

We can say something serious such as: "Because of who I am and what I believe, if I do my duty toward you and God, I need to try to persuade you to consider God, to consider the Scriptures and to come to Christ. But I don't know where to begin. If you were I, how would you talk to someone such as yourself about the Bible and Christ?"

It's important not to say anything more than this until the person answers. Sometimes a moment of silence will pass as the person processes your challenge and tries to fit it into the framework of his or her experience. Never be embarrassed by thoughtful reflection after a probing question.

The person may say, "It's impossible" or "It would be offensive." Accept that answer. Don't press the point. Don't drill holes in rock to plant gospel seed.

When you can't talk to your friend about God at a particular moment, you can certainly talk to God about your friend. **Prayer does make a difference in preparing hearts** to receive the message of the Messiah.

Wait for the right moment to reintroduce the subject. If the right moment never seems to come, keep praying. Realize that God can use your initial offer to that person as a seed that may bear fruit many years later.

On the other hand, the individual may say, "All right, I see that you feel you must explain your beliefs to me because it's your religious duty. I will listen to what you have to say."

Ask the person for about half an hour of his or her time. That is long enough to cover what you need to say, but not so long as to be grinding. Make an appointment to meet with the person later—do not jump into explaining the gospel at the moment they agree to talk.

Many Christians attempt to weave witnessing into the flow of everyday events. Of course, a person can pick up bits and pieces about God in this way. A witnessing situation **can** arise out of these casual encounters. However, we **must** communicate the substance and importance of conversion at a separate time that becomes a holy moment of receptivity. The person must be able to move into the mode of respectful listening as we change from ordinary conversation to holy explanation.

Consider a man courting a woman. What if he said to her, "Maybe next Tuesday night we can go to a movie. There are several that I would like to see. How is your friend Janie from college? Would you marry me? Maybe we could have the wedding in six months. One of the movies that I think you would like is 'Gone With the Wind.' Maybe Janie would like to come with us. Maybe she would like to be in the wedding."

Why would this man propose marriage in the middle of a mundane subject? A serious suitor would structure the situation. He might invite the woman to dinner and rehearse the dialogue. He might bring flowers and surprise her with a ring. He would try to create a special time. He would make it memorably different because the question is so important.

Likewise, how can we discuss how a person will spend eternity in the same way we talk about the latest football scores or fashion designs? When we begin to lead a person to Christ, we make an overture to the most serious matter in life. Witnessing is proposing—we propose on God's behalf!

Chapter Four
The Witnessing Appointment

The witnessing appointment can be on the telephone or in person—maybe in the individual's home or over coffee in a restaurant. But you need to change the setting so that your friend can move into a listening-hearing-learning mode. You must establish yourself as the teacher and the other person as the student.

Before you make the visit, think through, even rehearse, what you will say and how you will say it. Ask some Christian friends to pray for you. Then be certain to arrive for the witnessing appointment on time. Punctuality shows the serious nature of your endeavor.

The best kind of witnessing appointment takes place over an open Bible. In this way you have gained at least a modicum of respect for what you have to say even before you begin. Even if the person doesn't believe the Bible, he or she will know that you do and will listen more intently.

Open with a short prayer. Ask God to be present and to reveal Himself to your friend. Even a committed atheist will usually lower his gaze during such a prayer.

Do not take much time for small talk. Although you might compliment an appealing piece of art or a beautiful dress, move as quickly as you can to the Bible. I suggest you start in the Gospel of John.

Sin, Salvation and Savior

Establish the direction of the witness. Before reading from the Bible, frame the discussion with a good question such as: "Have you ever considered receiving Jesus as your Lord and Savior?" Don't press for an answer. Just allow the person to start thinking about the idea of belonging to Christ.

In going through John, make sure that the person understands these three essential elements: **Sin, Salvation and Savior.**

- **We must admit our sin.**
- **We must acknowledge that our sins have separated us from God and that we, therefore, need salvation.**
- **We must know that Jesus is the Savior and must ask Him to receive us as a repentant sinner.**

Start with John 1:11-12: "He came to His own, and His own did not receive Him. But as many as received Him, to them He gave the right to become children of God, even to those who believe in His name."

John 1:11 gives a reason why people don't receive Jesus, why they don't come to the light. Have the person to whom you are witnessing read the passage that says, "And this is the condemnation, that the light has come into the world, and men loved darkness rather than light, because their deeds were evil" (John 3:19). Link this to Romans 3:23, which says, "For all have sinned and fall short of the glory of God."

Explain that **"sin"** is not merely a **deed** but also a condition. Don't hesitate to read as much Scripture as necessary to explain sin. (See page 35 for a list of other verses you may find helpful.)

Turn to the verse: "He was in the world, and the world was made through Him, and the world did not know Him. He came to His own, and His own did not receive Him." Emphasize the word "receive" because this is what you're asking the person to do—**receive the Savior.** To "receive" is to make a commitment.

Some people will respond, "I heard this as a child. I never rejected it." Explain to them how "never rejecting" is not the same as **receiving.**

A person may or may not have made a decision for Christ as a child. He or she may have gone forward to the altar or said a silent prayer. However, if he lacks evidence of living for Y'shua, assume he did not properly understand that commitment.

Once a person comprehends what it means to receive—that totality of making a commitment—move on to the next verse in John which introduces **salvation** or the new birth: "Who were born, not of blood, nor of the will of the flesh nor of the will of man, <u>but of God</u>."

Refer to John 3:17-20 which explains that God has already **condemned the whole world.** The planet is useless. Discarded. God can find nothing worth saving in the world as it is. The curse of

Adam is on the planet—this is why we have eco-
logical problems. The curse of Adam is also on the
people—this is why we have personal problems.
We have served and pleased ourselves rather than
God. This is why we are condemned. This is why
we need salvation.

Read John 1:29 where it describes baptism.
Quote John as he says about Jesus, "Behold! The
Lamb of God who takes away the sin of the
world!" Link this point to Isaiah 53:6: "All we like
sheep have gone astray; we have turned, everyone,
to his own way; and the Lord has laid on Him the
iniquity of us all."

Many Christians start talking about hell at this
point. However, I have found people to be more
receptive when I connect the word "iniquity" with
the lamb. If we have already established that we
all are sinners, then we can easily point to a need
for a sacrificial lamb. This leads us into a discussion of the resurrection.

Refer to John 2:19-23 where Y'shua is at
Jerusalem during Passover:

> Jesus answered and said to them,
> "Destroy this temple, and in three days
> I will raise it up."
> Then the Jews said, "It has taken
> forty-six years to build this temple, and
> will You raise it up in three days?"
> But He was speaking of the temple
> of His body. Therefore, when He had

risen from the dead, His disciples remembered that He had said this to them; and they believed the Scriptures and the word which Jesus had said.

Now when He was in Jerusalem at the Passover, during the feast, many believed inHis name when they saw the signs which He did.

This passage shows the Jewishness of Jesus, which will interest Jewish people in particular.

Let's next turn to John 3:14 where Jesus said, "And as Moses lifted up the serpent in the wilderness, so must the Son of Man be lifted up." He was not talking about being exalted; He was talking about the picture of death by crucifixion. The serpent in the wilderness was a symbol of judgment. Death by execution was a symbol of judgment for all sin.

Death on the cross represents a lonely, ignominious end and humanity's destiny without Christ. However, the next passage offers the way out, "That whoever believes in Him should not perish but have eternal life. For God so loved the world that He gave His only begotten son that **whoever....**"

Explain it this way: "The 'whoever' is the person who chooses to believe. Perhaps the better word is 'trust.' God wants you to believe in Him and trust Him. He wants you to have the joy of belonging to Him."

Don't be afraid to tell people what God expects of them. As long as you can back it up in Scripture, it will carry the authority that it needs and deserves.

At this point a person should be able to see and acknowledge his or her sin, the need for salvation and the person of Jesus as Savior.

Ask if he can see what he needs to be saved from. Ask if he wants things to be different. Describe what will happen. Tell him that because of sin we cannot see spiritual truths in our own ability. Our sinful nature clouds our perception. But when we receive the "new birth," we are born again with the power to see the Kingdom of God.

God infuses us with new life! A metaphor could help right here. Explain that our lives naturally run on bad fuel. And our engines have major defects. They get clogged. Some backfire, some stall and some explode. All end up broken down and in the junkyard. God wants to put in each of us a new motor that runs on His fuel and lasts forever. His salvation is not merely a tune-up, it is a complete overhaul with both new fuel and a new engine.

State very clearly that if we want this new life, we must turn to the Messiah for salvation and regeneration.

What Comes After the Gospel?

Once we present the basic gospel, we must draw back. Give the person a chance to think over what we have said. How we handle ourselves at this moment can determine how much a person feels he or she can open up to us in the future.

In witnessing, we must help people without manipulating them. We maintain integrity by the way we postulate or set forth an assumption. We keep communication channels open by not pushing or forcing a person to make a decision. There is a difference between motivating and shoving.

Other verses on sin

Original Sin: Genesis 3:6; Romans 5:12, 15-19.

Sin Nature: Matthew 7:17; Matthew 12:33-35; Luke 6:45; Romans 7:17,20,23,25; Galatians 5:16-17; James 1:14.

Sin as Transgression: Hosea 6:8; 1 Corinthians 8:12; James 2:10.

Sin as Turning Away From God: Psalm 95:10.

Sin as Not Seeking God: 2 Chronicles 12:14.

Sin as Lack of Faith: Romans 14:23.

Other Verses on Sin: 2 Samuel 12:14; Psalm 119:113; Amos 9:2-4; Matthew 23:33; Luke 12:2; John 8:34; Romans 6:16; Hebrews 2:1-3; 2 Peter 2:19; Revelation 22:3-4.

The person to whom you witness will likely have doubts—if not about God, certainly about the Bible and the person of Christ. When doubts arise, get the person to look at his or her own behavioral patterns. Ask him to recall his doubts about other decisions in life such as which college he attended, which profession he chose and which house he purchased.

Let him know that God doesn't say, "Don't doubt, don't ask." Consider the intimacy with which Jesus regards Thomas when He says, "Put your hand in my side, in my wounds. See that they're real." He allows His disciples personal privileges with His own body to assuage their hesitations and fears.

A person may cite the ugliness of the televangelists' scandals as a reason for disbelief. This gives you a great opportunity to witness. Explain that the fact of "scandal" indicates that Christianity has standards of conduct. Acknowledge that Christian standards are very high and that sometimes Christian leaders fail to achieve them. Tell the person that scandals show the need for everyone to lead a holy life—something no one can do unless he has a savior who will forgive sin.

Don't apologize for or justify the scandals— use them as a stepping stone to talk about sin and how God forgives. After all, we don't preach the righteousness of God's ministers. We preach that God is righteous and requires holy lives. Don't malign the teacher merely because his student fails to learn. It could be that a student failed to pay attention to the teaching. Don't think that a law is bad because people break it.

Whatever reason a person gives for doubt—the holocaust, evil in the world, the failures of Christians—just remember that unbelief is natural. Don't allow sidetracks such as these to distract you into apologizing for anything or anyone. Focus on God and His works.

Moreover, don't despise **honest** skepticism. A skeptic might ask a question that needs to be answered. Such questions can help you organize your thinking. The answers will motivate and move ahead the person to whom you are witnessing. However, when you first present the gospel, entertain only the questions to which you can provide solid answers at the moment. Postpone all other answers to a later time.

The Trap of Non-Commitment

If the witnessing process moves along smoothly, the person may be ready to acknowledge their need for Christ at this point. However, they may not be willing to make a commitment even if they don't have any solid arguments against Christ. By habit, most people simply don't allow someone else to lead them. That way they can avoid coming to any conclusion. Perhaps the most characteristic flaw of modern man is terminal inconclusiveness. Daniel Berrigan said, "Not to decide is to decide already."

The person to whom you witness may not even be able to understand how he or she is a sinner—or at least may not be willing to admit it. This is typical of the non-decisive, non-committal type of person. As part of their social armor, these usually intelligent people defer making any kind of commitment until they see the immediate need or benefit for themselves. Because of the benefits, they commit themselves to marriage, to college, to finding a place to live.

We need to explain to a non-committal type of person that commitment to God is different. We do not accept God's benefit plan; we accept Christ.

How can we recognize a non-committal type of person? Invite him to a meal. Ask him where he would like to eat dinner. The classic non-committal type will bounce the choice back to you. He likely fears making a decision or doesn't want to go against your preference. The classic non-committal type of person, however, will always reserve a veto right. If we suggest Chinese food, but he doesn't like Chinese food, he will likely say, "Oh, I ate at a Hunan restaurant two days ago," or "I'm sorry, Chinese food disagrees with me."

You need to help the person with the non-committal behavior syndrome. He has likely gotten into the habit of going with the flow of whatever is happening, then balking when it comes to making a decision. He needs to see that he must act, exert his own will and exercise his own intentions.

You can help such a person get over the hurdle of decision-making. Have him assume a position for the sake of understanding it. Get him to agree that there can only be a "yes" or "no" answer to certain questions. Ask him to yield just for the sake of this conversation even if he doesn't fully agree with what you present to be true. By assuming in this manner, he will become more comfortable with speculative discussion. It will also avoid non-committal "maybes" that bog down the witnessing process. Let him see that anything that leads us to wait when we ought to act, hurts.

In setting forth a proposition, you might ask, "Can you allow the possibility that Christ lived, that He talked, that He did miracles, and that He died for your sins? Yes or no?" The non-committal person might say, "Well, maybe He was a good man, but...." Don't accept the "but" as part of the answer. Ask him to assume a position now and clarify the "buts" and "maybes" later.

Tell It Like It Is

God requires much. It may be hard at first, but we must let the person know this. If a person is a thief and wants to go on being a thief, he or she can't really come to Jesus. Jesus tells us to steal no more and to restore what we have stolen. If the person habitually lies, there must be repentance.

Moreover, repentance means turning 180 degrees around and going the other direction. The person to whom you witness must understand this.

Don't promote the wrong doctrine which some call "easy-believism." When we talk with someone about their sin we can ask, "Do you regret this? Do you want things to be different? Are you willing to give up the bad attitude that led you to bad actions? Do you believe that God can give you the strength to make things different? Will you commit yourself into the hands of God to make that difference in your life? Do you believe that Christ rose from the dead? Yes or no? Not maybe. Can you give me one reason why you shouldn't pray to receive Him as your Savior right now?"

We must be careful and precise to see that the person knows what we mean by the gospel. People talk about "gospel music" and "the gospel according to so- and-so." Make sure the person knows that you are talking about the gospel according to God.

After we adequately explain the meaning of sin, savior and salvation, we need to assist people in moving forward in their thinking.

If we present the gospel and the person comprehends it, then we can seek closure to our presentation by asking the person to receive the Lord as Savior.

Scripture clearly and firmly states that we must stand upon our convictions. First Corinthians 15:1-3 reads, "Moreover, brethren, I declare to you the gospel which I preached to you, which also you received and in which you stand, by which also you are saved, if you hold fast that word which I preached to you—unless you believed in vain. For I delivered to you first of all that which I also received: that Christ died for our sins according to the Scriptures... ."

After reading this verse, we can ask the person: "Have you discovered that Jesus died for your sins?" If they say, "Yes," then we have an open door. We should ask them, "What do you want to do about it?"

Do not presume that because a person knows about the crucifixion and forgiveness he or she is saved.

How do we know when to ask a person to make a decision for Christ? During the witnessing process we should be reading from the Bible. Get the person to read some passages as well. We can augment the Gospel of John with a few other related verses. Watch how he reacts to the Word of God. If he gladly receives it and obviously wants to know more, then he is ready to make a faith commitment.

However, **do not rush the process.** Don't overwhelm him or her with too many verses or too much information. If the person is resisting major portions of what we say, then we must pull back. Suggest another meeting. Give some homework and offer some questions for him to ponder. Be assured that as we leave the person, the Holy Spirit doesn't.

If the person understands there is a whole life he or she has not been able to experience because of sin—but wants to—he is ready for the next important step: Get him to return to the text of John 1:12. Then ask: "Are you ready to receive Jesus now and to become God's child through the new birth?"

If the answer is "yes," then explain the prayer of repentance in terms the person can recognize. Too many Christians fumble through this part of witnessing, presuming that the person knows what commitment means, or afraid they will recoil if they know exactly what they are committing themselves to.

Like a Marriage

I like this explanation: The new birth is not like the first birth. Our first birth was a natural event over which we had no choice. The new birth is a supernatural event that requires us to choose. In this it is more like a marriage than a birth.

Say something such as: "God wants you to belong to Him and He wants to belong to you. He wants you to be His person, and He wants to be your Lord and Savior. He wants your love freely, and He wants your obedience to be because of that love. It's something like a marriage. He's been waiting for you. He's been wanting you. He has always loved you and now has proposed this relationship. It's up to you to say, 'YES!'"

As in a marriage proposal, God asks, "Will you be mine?"

An Army of Peacemakers

If the metaphor of marriage is inappropriate, try another example of commitment. Compare making a decision for Christ to enlisting in the military.

Try saying something such as: "God is calling on you to be part of the army of the Prince of Peace whose sword is the Word of God. Join His army of peacemakers."

Just as an army looks after its own, in the church we have comrades who care for us. We also have a commander who looks after our welfare and provides for our strength. Even so, when God is your commander, He strengthens you by His Holy Spirit and provides all you need. Furthermore, He sends you into places of victory!

Just as an army must provide the training to enable its members to accomplish a military purpose, God provides training so that His followers can achieve a messianic purpose. As an army has a quartermaster corps, a transportation corps and every other kind of corps necessary to provide for its soldiers in the fields, so God supports those who enlist in His army. Moreover, He goes before us. When we're truly following Him, we are unbeatable, invincible.

This can start to sound like Christian jargon. So explain the places of victory God has taken you and where He can take the person to whom you are witnessing.

Citizens of Heaven

Another useful metaphor is citizenship. When we come to the Lord we must accept citizenship in heaven. We become aliens to the planet where we were born. However, we have a divine visa. We must still observe and obey the laws of the land unless they contradict the higher laws of God.

We must speak the language of the land, but there's a higher language. On earth we are ordinary people, commoners, unrecognized. However, as citizens of heaven we become noble, in fact royal.

Sometimes people leave their native countries to emigrate to faraway places. Sometimes they must give up all of their resources, including their home and prized possessions. When they arrive in their new nations, often they live in poverty or struggle to survive. Usually those who leave their place of nativity do so to gain a freedom or an opportunity to better exercise their abilities and fulfill their rightful ambitions. The same is true when we choose to emigrate to heaven. We give up much to gain something better.

When the time is right, don't hesitate to urge: "Are you ready for something better? Are you ready to pray?" If you don't have a prayer memorized, you may want to lead the person in saying this one:

> "God of Abraham, I know that I
> have sinned against You, and I want to
> turn from my sins.
> I believe You provided Jesus
> [Y'shua when witnessing to Jews] as a
> once-and-for-all atonement for me.
> With this prayer, I receive
> Jesus as my Savior and my Lord. I
> thank You for cleansing me of sin and
> making me a new person. Amen!"

After a person has accepted Christ, there must be follow-up. The most important things to remember are:

• If the person makes a commitment to Christ, explain what that commitment means. Tell him that he might not feel different, that the "new birth" is a direction as well as a decision. Urge him to begin moving. Make certain he understands that we start the motion and God helps us progress.

• Get new believers involved in regular Bible reading. Try to meet with them to study the Bible together. If that is not practical, offer to call on the telephone and read some passages together on a daily basis for a few weeks.

• Pray with the person. This helps him or her learn how to talk with God.

• Urge the new believer to tell someone about his commitment to Christ. This can be a family member, a friend or a pastor. It is important to actualize Romans 10:9-10: "That if you confess with your mouth the Lord Jesus and believe in your heart that God has raised Him from the dead, you will be saved. For with the heart one believes to righteousness, and with the mouth confession is made to salvation."

• Encourage the person to fellowship. No matter how committed you are to the individual, you can't be the whole body of Christ to him or her.

You can't meet all the person's spiritual needs. A new believer must meet and know other Christians. As a way to get started, invite him to your church or get him to attend a church similar to yours.

The old hymn captures it so well: *There is joy in serving Jesus.* Perhaps the greatest satisfaction in life comes when we see others love Y'shua because we love Him and love others.

Helping people to love was a career for Jesus. You can make a career out of helping people love Him, no matter how you earn a living. It will delight you when some of your friends, neighbors and co-workers come to love Him and serve Him because you do.

N

60
San Francisco,
(415) 864-